Copyright © 2023 by Noel Warnell

*All rights reserved. No part of this publication may be reproduced, stored or transmitted in any form or by any means, electronic, mechanical, photocopying, recording, scanning, or otherwise without written permission from the publisher. It is illegal to copy this book, post it to a website, or distribute it by any other means without permission.*

*Noel Warnell asserts the moral right to be identified as the author of this work.*

*Designations used by companies to distinguish their products are often claimed as trademarks. All brand names and product names used in this book and on its cover are trade names, service marks, trademarks and registered trademarks of their respective owners. The publishers and the book are not associated with any product or vendor mentioned in this book. None of the companies referenced within the book have endorsed the book.*

*First edition published April 2023*

# The Quarterly Agile Planning Journal

Copyright © (Noel Warnell 2023)
All Rights Reserved

No part of this book may be reproduced in any form by photocopying or any electronic or mechanical means including information storage or retrieval systems, without permission in writing from both the copyright owner and publisher of the book.

ISBN: 9781804673652
Perfect Bound

First published in 2023 by bookvault Publishing, Peterborough, United Kingdom

An Environmentally friendly book printed and bound in England by bookvault, powered by printondemand-worldwide

# QUARTERLY AGILE PLANNING JOURNAL

Helping you stay organised & deliver with confidence, calm and clarity

Noel Warnell

*"Write the book you wish to read, the one you cannot find."*
Carol Shields

*"Knowledge is not enough; it must be applied. Willing is not enough; we must do."*
Vint Cerf

*"Explore. Dream. Discover."*
Mark Twain

This book is for people who organise and run Quarterly Agile Planning

It is designed to help you design, execute, reflect on, and continuously improve quarterly agile planning.

It provides a sprint by sprint breakdown of key events, templates, ideas and articles to support you becoming a quarterly planning ninja.

# This is not just a book, it's a journal too.

It should end up
bursting with your own
notes, doodles,
ideas, and observations

This book is not perfect, so use it as your guide. Don't feel constrained, feel inspired.

# Contents

Introduction ............................................................. 13
An overview ............................................................ 15
How to use the journal ............................................ 14
What about Kanban? ............................................... 19
S.T.A.T.I.K. visual .................................................... 21
  How to use the journal ......................................... 22
Q1 ............................................................................. 25
Sprint 1 .................................................................... 27
    Scrum of Scrums / Team Coach Sync ............... 30
    Product Sync ......................................................... 31
    Product Management .......................................... 33
    Product Owner Bullseye! .................................... 35
    Team Retrospective ............................................. 36
    Team Review ........................................................ 37
    System Demo ....................................................... 38
Sprint 2 .................................................................... 39
    Communities of practice .................................... 42
    Metrics, Data & Reporting ................................. 45
    Things you could measure and include in reporting ... 46
    Book Summary - The Balanced Scorecard.. ... 48
    Book Summary - Accelerate ............................. 50
    Book Summary - Succeeding with OKRs in Agile ... 52
    Team Health Check ............................................ 54
Sprint 3 .................................................................... 59
    Business Alignment ............................................ 63
    Value Stream Mapping ....................................... 65

- What is Team Topologies? ... 70
  - Book Summary - Team Topologies ... 71
- Sprint 4 ... 73
  - Funding Allocation ... 77
- Sprint 5 ... 79
- Wrap up & Reset ... 83
  - Quarterly Business Review ... 86
  - Quarterly Retrospective ... 90
  - Experiment Canvas ... 91
  - The Main Event ... 93
  - Pecha Kucha visual ... 97
  - Quarterly Planning ... 99
- Planning Event Checklists for:
  - You! ... 100
  - Scrum Masters / Team Coaches ... 101
  - Product Owners ... 102
  - Team Members ... 103
  - Tech Leadership / System Architect ... 104
  - Product Managers ... 105
- Q2 ... 106
- Q3 ... 130
- Q4 ... 154
- What's Next? ... 179
- Author Bio ... 183

# Introduction

**This Quarterly Agile Planning Journal is for Release Train Engineers, Agile Coaches, Lean Portfolio Managers, and anyone else with a weird job title that's responsible for organising and running quarterly agile planning cycles.**

It's designed purely to help you organise, execute, reflect on and continuously improve your planning intervals, by providing a sprint by sprint notebook, detailing key events and sharing templates, ideas and articles to support you becoming a quarterly planning ninja.

As a scrum master, a release train engineer, and an agile coach I've supported over 100 quarterly planning events for multiple clients, across a variety of sectors, geographies and maturity levels. I'm not a SAFe Program Consultant (never have been and never will be), and have no intention of opening a debate on any of the scaling frameworks by producing this journal.

**Small is always better when it comes to agile planning, and it's actually extremely rare that a full scaling solution is truly needed to build, measure and learn from product development.**

The intention of the journal is simply to share hands-on experience to make the planning, executing, reflecting on and improving these events a little easier for those that find themselves involved in, or helping to coordinate them.

This is the journal I wish I had when given responsibility to organise and run a quarterly planning process for 8 teams. This is the missing guide that would have stopped me flapping about, and help focus my attention in the right direction.

It supports four full quarters, so could become a must have requirement for your work bag or desk for the next 12 months.

The journal makes the following assumptions:

- You're familiar with Scrum and the concept of 2 week sprints
- You have multiple teams that are interdependent to deliver a product or service
- As multiple teams are involved there are single team events and others that support multiple teams.
- Each quarterly planning cycle is six sprints / iterations of two weeks. So, each section covers 12 weeks.
- The last sprint is focused on reflection of the quarter, and planning for the next (for those of you using the SAFe framework this is the innovation and planning bit).

The journal starts with an overview of a full end to end planning cycle, it will then break down each sprint in detail, and provide tips every step of the way. Make sure you read the 'How to use the journal' section before jumping in.

Along the way there's a bunch of notes for the different events, but this is not 'official' guidance, it's simply my thoughts as an experienced practitioner.

To get the full benefit of **The Quarterly Agile Planning Journal** you'll need to make this YOUR journal. It should end up being 40% of provided content and 60% yours, (most of my stuff is spread through the Q1 section). If you stick with it, by the time you reach the end it will be bursting with your notes, doodles, insights, experiments, which together tell the fascinating story of a year in the life of your career.

Go forth and plan with clarity, calm and confidence my friend, I've got your back.

Noel.

# An Overview

I doubt you're underestimating the amount of work required to design and run a successful quarterly agile planning cycle...but just in case...

The job requires you to be a:

- Salesperson
- Event planner
- Facilitator
- Public speaker
- Toastmaster
- Party host
- Coach
- Teacher
- Mentor
- Leader
- Referee
- Concerned Parent
- Blocker /
- Unblocker
- Journalist / Presentation creator
- Good and Bad cop
- Scientist
- Juggler

Wow. That's quite a list.

I'm not putting it here to freak you out. It's to remind you what an incredible opportunity this is. This can truly be the catalyst you've been waiting for to accelerate your visibility and career.

It can of course feel overwhelming figuring out when to put on the right hat and how to fit all of this into a 3 month cycle, especially when you're just getting started. But don't be daunted. That's what this journal is all about. To guide you and provide comfort in synchronously managing multiple tracks (readiness, execution, reflection and improvement), across multiple flight levels (operational, co-ordinating and strategic).

Your role needs to be centred on guiding the members of the system towards the delivery of value, and over each 3 month cycle you'll have plenty of time to achieve this. You just need to be deliberate in your approach, pace yourself, and have a clear schedule that you can organise yourself and others around.

**Each quarter will typically look like the overview below, but I encourage you to make this your own over time.**

# You should have the autonomy to tailor the design of the quarter to best suit the needs of your context and organisation.

Please use this journal as a guide. Not as a holy grail.

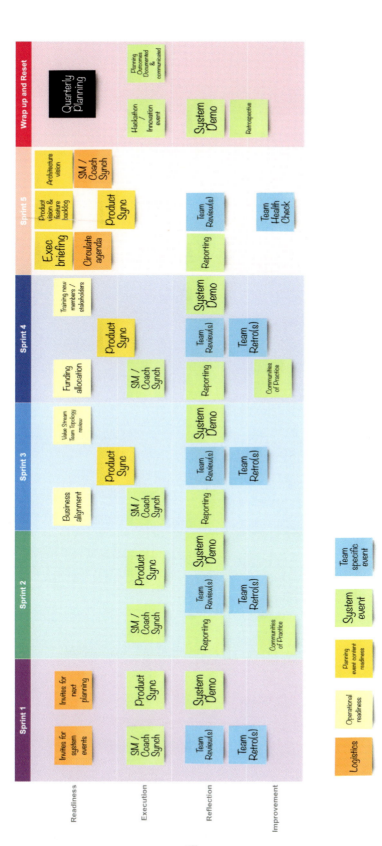

# What about Kanban?

You may have noticed that Scrum was referenced in the assumptions section but the Kanban Method was not. This is because in my experience Kanban is significantly less prevalent than Scrum when it comes to scaling agile.

## But, if you're not familiar with, or using the Kanban method, then I absolutely encourage you to explore applying it.

Its six general practices are entirely relevant to working with a system of multiple interdependent teams.

1. **Visualise** - Providing regular reporting, having information radiators available in office spaces and working 'in the open' as much as possible should be commonplace (this is how I took this to the extreme!)

2. **Limit WIP** - Smaller batch sizes means faster flow. FACT.

3. **Manage flow** - determine cost of delay & classes of service

4. **Make policies explicit** - create empowering constraints, like definition of ready for quarterly planning

5. **Feedback loops** - get 'frequent enough' meetings in place to ensure open communication and opportunities for feedback are available

6. **Evolve & Improve** - experiment, and aim for continuous and incremental change

How do you go about introducing Kanban? Use the S.T.A.T.I.K. technique...

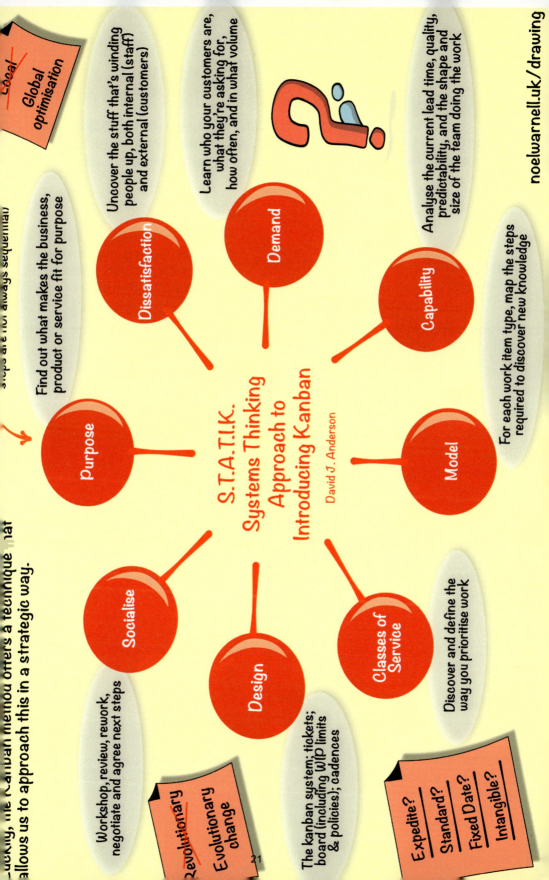

# How to use the journal

Every sprint has a 2 page spread with plenty of space to add your notes. Crucially, it includes different sections for readiness, execution, reflection and improvement activities. In each section there's also a sprint specific checklist.

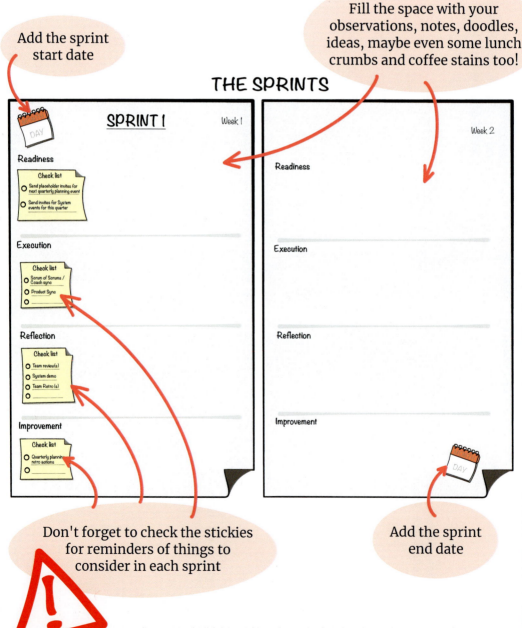

Add the sprint start date

Fill the space with your observations, notes, doodles, ideas, maybe even some lunch crumbs and coffee stains too!

Don't forget to check the stickies for reminders of things to consider in each sprint

Add the sprint end date

In the Q1 section, you'll find some extra notes and guidance relevant to the activities that take place within each sprint.
This could be written content, event cards, detailed checklists, or even visual book summaries.

*Download these for free at www.noelwarnell.uk/QAP*

## EVENT CARDS

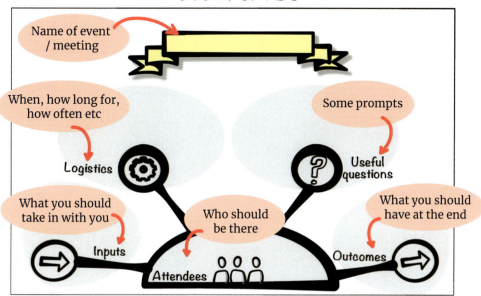

## PLANNING EVENT CHECKLISTS

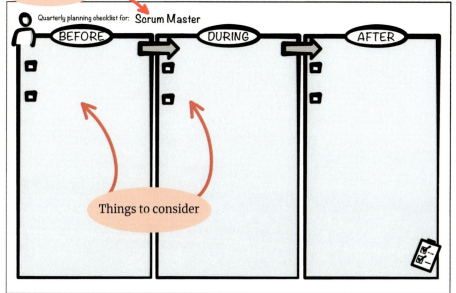

*"Organisations that consistently engage in quarterly planning are better able to align their resources and focus on what matters most, which ultimately leads to better outcomes."*

The Value of Quarterly Planning Cycles, Harvard Business Review, August 2018.

# SPRINT 1

# SPRINT 1

Week 1

## Readiness

**Check list**
- ○ Send placeholder invites for next quarterly planning event
- ○ Send invites for System events for this quarter

## Execution

**Check list**
- ○ Scrum of Scrums / Coach sync
- ○ Product Sync
- ○ _____

## Reflection

**Check list**
- ○ Team review(s)
- ○ System demo
- ○ Team Retro (s)
- ○ _____

## Improvement

**Check list**
- ○ Quarterly planning retro actions
- ○ _____

Week 2

Readiness

Execution

Reflection

Improvement

# SCRUM of SCRUMS / TEAM COACH SYNC

**Logistics**
- At least once per sprint
- 30 mins
- Focus on execution of quarter goals / objectives
- Facilitated by you!

**Useful questions**
- What's slowing you down?
- Who are you waiting for?
- What hypothesis are you currently testing?

**Attendees**
- Team coaches
- Scrum masters

**Inputs**
- Risks, issues, dependencies & blockers

**Outcomes**
- Shared understanding & alignment
- Collective focus

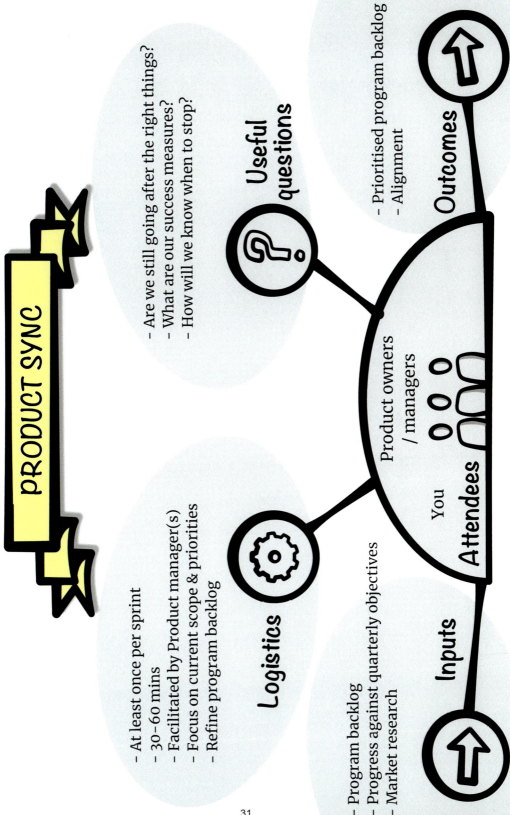

# Product Management

*"Things which matter most must never be at the mercy of things which matter least."*
Johann Wolfgang Von Goethe

**Organisations that build products should have a dedicated product management function. These people create and hold the vision of the product they want and why they want it.**

What they often lack is a balance between capability (people, time, or money) and the demand they create. So when it comes to quarterly planning the constant challenge is deciding what's next (and what not to do) considering the constraints.

Hence, it's critical to have a consistent prioritisation method and a living product roadmap. This helps review and rank potential work items considering the cost (money, opportunity) vs value (productivity, increased market adoption). This is where the Product Sync comes in.

Some good questions to ask include:

- What problem are we trying to solve? Why are we building the product?
- Who is for? Who benefits from this product?
- What difference will it make?
- What's most important? Building the right thing, building it right, or building it fast?
- Who are the real stakeholders?
- What can get us learning fastest? Prototype / Wireframes / Customer research?
- How best to create a backlog that gives the most value?

There are a metric crap tonne[1] of prioritisation models out there, and you probably already have something in place.

---

[1] There's 100 craploads in 1 crap tonne. There's 100 crap tonnes in a shitload and 100 shitloads in a shit tonne.

But, just in case this is a new function for you, and you need some direction here's a list of some popular options:

- R.I.C.E. (Reach, Impact, Confidence, Effort)
- Value vs Effort
- Kano Model
- Story Mapping
- MoSCoW
- Cost of Delay
- WSJF (Weighted Shortest Job First)
- Eisenhower Decision Matrix

You can google search any of these (go to the images view for a quick understanding), and get the details of how they work.

Finally, when it comes to ensuring the product team is synchronised there should also be a discussion about leading (predictive) and lagging (output driven) indicators i.e. once a new product or feature is in the hands of a customer, how will you know it's providing the value you were aiming for? What measurable signal, or data is going to give you this insight?

Having an aligned product team, with a clear vision and roadmap is essential to successful quarterly agile planning.

I highly recommend having a clearly defined definition of ready for your quarterly agile planning, and refusing to allow any work that doesn't meet these standards.

Keep this conversation alive throughout the quarter. If you don't, there's a high risk of the product team trying to force work that is simply not defined well enough into the teams.

**This is the most common reason I've seen for quarterly agile planning being derailed. You have been warned!**

To understand the maturity of the Product team you're working with, why not facilitate a conversation by playing PO Bullseye?

# Product Owner Bullseye!

**Purpose:**
- To visualise the point in time truth for the product owners you're working with
- To gently remind the product owners of some basic good practise

**Instructions:**
- Give your product owners stickers (different colour for each)
- Simply ask them "what is true for you?"
- Product owners put a sticker on the line for each question with the yellow centre being 'this is totally true for me', and the grey outer circle being 'this is not currently true for me'.

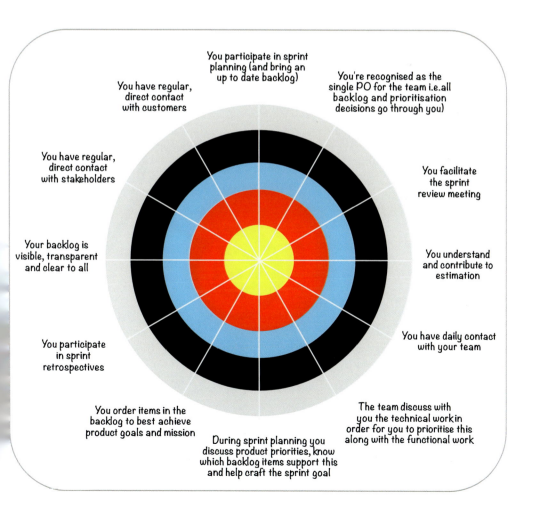

Miro template can be dowloaded for free: noelwarnell.uk/QAP

# TEAM RETROSPECTIVE

**Useful questions**
- How's the human connection in the team?
- What's wound you up?
- What surprised you?
- What's not being said?

**Logistics**
- Once per sprint, on final day
- Facilitated by Scrum master, coach or you
- 60–90 mins
- Figure out how to increase quality, collaboration and team effectiveness

**Attendees**
- Product owner
- Dev team

**Inputs**
- Assumptions made
- Successes & failures
- Dependencies & blockers
- Insights from team review

**Outcomes**
- Improvement actions (with owners)

# TEAM REVIEW

## Useful questions

- What value were you focussed on providing?
- Who cares most about the work completed?
- Any blockers that impacted the iteration?
- Any dependencies needing close management?

## Logistics

- Once per sprint, on final day
- 30 – 60 mins
- Facilitated by product owner with your support
- Share progress against Sprint goal and quarterly objectives

## Attendees

- Dev team
- Product owner / manager
- System Architect

## Outcomes

- Content for System demo
- Stakeholder feedback
- Data for reporting
- Transparency

## Inputs

- Iteration / sprint goal
- Feature & story backlog
- Team capacity
- Flow metrics

# SYSTEM DEMO

**Useful questions**
- Did we build the best product?
- What support do we need?
- Do we truly understand our customer personas?

**Logistics**
- Once, at the end of each sprint & quarter
- 60 mins
- Facilitated by you, with product leading the demo
- Demonstrate product development

**Attendees**
EVERYONE!

**Inputs**
- Product vision
- Insights from team reviews

**Outcomes**
- Transparency
- Alignment
- Excitement!

# SPRINT 2

# SPRINT 2

Week 1

## Readiness

**Check list**
- Next quarterly planning event venue / meeting room booking
- _____

## Execution

**Check list**
- Scrum of Scrums / Coach sync
- Product Sync
- _____

## Reflection

**Check list**
- Team review(s)
- System demo
- Team Retro (s)
- Reporting

## Improvement

**Check list**
- Quarterly planning retro actions
- Team retro actions
- Communities of practice

# Week 2

Readiness

Execution

Reflection

Improvement

# COMMUNITY OF PRACTICE

### Useful questions
- What experiments can you try?
- What organisation challenges can you attempt to solve?
- How do you advance your craft?

### Logistics
- Frequency determined by the group
- Facilitated by the group, with support from you
- Voluntary attendance
- Focus on exchanging knowledge & skills

### Attendees
Open membership

### Inputs
- Growth mindset
- Shared area of interest
- Shared body of knowledge

### Outcomes
- Connected employees
- Increased domain maturity
- Faster problem solving

# 11 Facilitation Ideas for Communities of Practice

When a group of people with experience in a common domain and a growth mindset volunteer to come together, you've got yourself a community of practice. But something to watch out for is the discussions becoming a bit circular and people leaving the sessions without anything tangible. Here's some ideas to prevent that happening:

- **Blocker clustering** - create a list of role or domain specific blockers the group have faced. Group, discuss and prioritise them. Share mitigation strategies.

- **Create a retro** - collaborate to co-design a format for a retrospective to run with development teams, that would shine a light on your role / domain. Find volunteers in the group willing to facilitate it with the teams

- **Facilitation lab** - a space to experiment with facilitation ideas, untried workshops, activities and receive feedback from the group before trying it out 'for real'

- **Triz**[1] - Stop counterintuitive activities and behaviours to make space for innovation

- **Book review** - after reading a book relevant to the CoP, the reader would summarise their key takeaways and present them to the group. You could also run this as a book club, where multiple people read the same book at the same time and then share their key gripe and key insight afterwards.

---

[1] https://www.liberatingstructures.com/6-making-space-with-triz/

- **Lean coffee**[2] - democratically generate and prioritise an agenda, then start talking!

- **Coaching/ Mentoring dojo** - explore the skills of role / domain specific coaching and mentoring and how you can provide this as a service for the wider organisation

- **Troika consulting**[3] - get immediate help from the CoP for existing challenges / issues

- **What does good look like?** - use the miracle question to ideate the ideal future "If you woke up tomorrow and the role / domain was exactly what you wanted it to be, what is happening? Who would notice? What would they notice?

- **Blog together** - co-create written content about your role / domain that can be shared more widely

- **Failure spotlight** - this is last because it requires a degree of psychological safety within the group. Encourage people to share their failures with the intent to help others in the group avoid the same mistakes

Finally, another book recommendation: **Building Successful Communities of Practice** - Emily Webber[4]

---

[2] https://leancoffee.org/
[3] https://www.liberatingstructures.com/8-troika-consulting/
[4] https://hellotacit.com/tools/

# Metrics, Data & Reporting

A key responsibility when organising and running quarterly agile planning is to demonstrate progress, or not, in order to course correct.

To know whether to pivot, persevere, or even pause you need empirical insights. The challenge is to figure out what data is actually important in your context.

The best test for this is to see what data triggers decision making. If there's a bunch of data being captured and reported but nothing happens as a result, then why bother? So what?

## Find the stuff that people care about and react to, (yourself included), and make it visible.

To give you plenty of options, included next are:

- a mind map of '*Things you could measure & include in reporting*'
- a book summary of **The Balanced Scorecard** by Kaplan and Norton
- a book summary of **Accelerate: Building and Scaling Performing Technology Organisations** by Nicole Forsgren, Jez Humble and Gene Kim
- a book summary of **Succeeding with OKR's in Agile** by Allan Kelly

It's also worth spending some time on team health checks, an often forgotten concept that can have a real impact on organisational culture. So, more of that is coming up too.

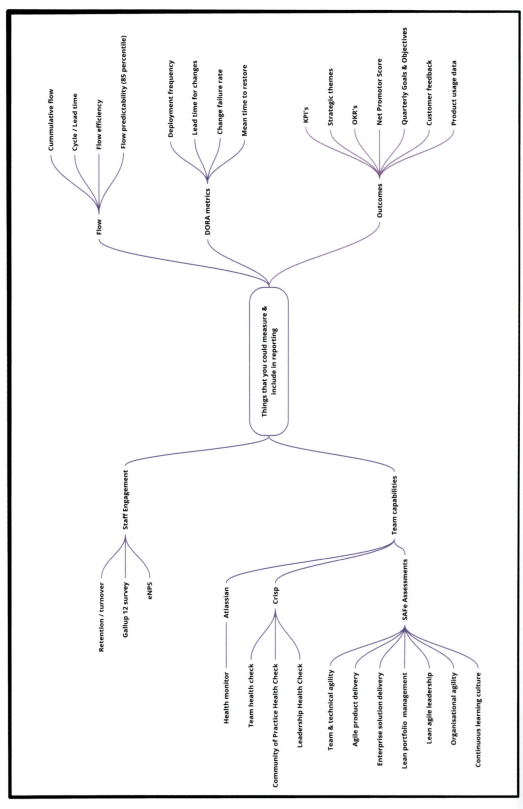

# What makes a Balanced Scorecard?

## Customer
Measures customer satisfaction & performance metrics

- ★ Retention rate?
- ★ Lifetime value?
- ★ Net Promoter Score?
- ★ Monthly Revenue?
- ★ Churn rate?

## Internal process
Measures critical (to-customer) processes

- Cycle time?
- Cost of delivery?
- Cost of delay?

— **Strategic Goals** — What are we aiming for?

## Financial
Tracks financial measures and performance

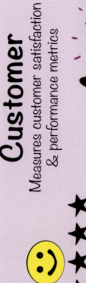

- Return on Investment?
- Revenue growth?
- Gross margin?
- Cost reduction?
- Forecast vs target?

Where are we going?

## Learning
Focus on people, engagement, & growth

- Knowledge
- Skills
- Employee engagement surveys
- Training
- Reflection
- Plan / Do / Check / Act

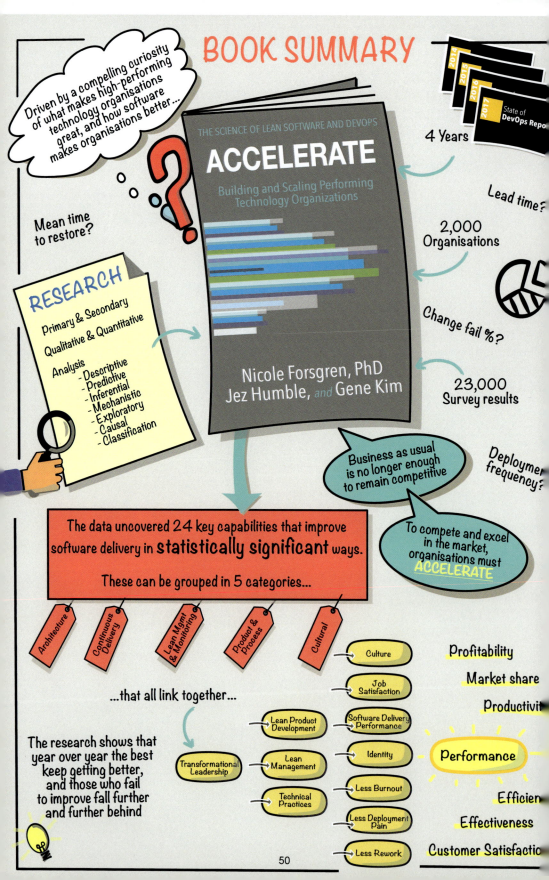

# Team Health Check

My preference for a number of years has been to run some kind of 'Health check' with teams every 3 months, capturing the results as data and forming an empirical baseline to track movement against. When doing this for multiple teams working in the same domain over time you'll naturally start to observe trends and adopt a more system thinking approach. There's a bunch of templates available for this online.[1]

When recently asking the agile community a question about this topic, my good friend Tobias Mayer shocked me with the following statement:

> *"What is a "team health check"? I've not heard that term before. Is that where the scrum master sticks thermometers in people's mouths, records their pulse and taps their knee with a hammer?"*

Bear in mind that Tobias has been an agile practitioner for 20 years, studied and taught Certified Scrum Master classes with Ken Schwaber in 2005, and in 2008 was the creative director for the Scrum Alliance. So when someone like that provokes you, it's good to listen. Ultimately in the discussion that followed Tobias' assertion was that this kind of conversation / format should already be built into Scrum through retrospectives, it shouldn't need to be a 'special' event.

Whether you do this as part of a retrospective, or run it as something different, the outcome remains the same - gathering insights and data on a regular basis so that an empirical approach can be applied.

---

[1] https://blog.crisp.se/2019/03/11/jimmyjanlen/health-checks-for-teams-and-leadership
https://www.atlassian.com/team-playbook/health-monitor
https://scaledagileframework.com/measure-and-grow/

Another friend and seasoned Agile coach - Greg Franklin, did an excellent job of explaining his approach in this 2023 LinkedIn article[2].

---

For a few years, I have been developing my own approach in evaluating what I call 'team awesomeness' and people seem very interested in how I do it. It may seem straightforward or a box-ticking exercise, but there are a couple of key factors that really make it impactful.

## Make the evaluation meaningful

To start with, the self-scoring statements should be relevant and important to the teams filling out the survey. I do this by drawing on Lean-Agile principles, themes of diversity and inclusion, psychological safety, as well as company values in the context of the teams filling out the survey.
I like to run the questionnaire with cross-functional software teams, but it can be adapted for any type of team. I usually run them every 3-6 months, and compare the team with their former selves. Never compare a team to other teams!

The purpose of the survey is not to report to management but for the team to improve - it is important to communicate this to the individuals filling out the survey.

## Design the survey for meaningful visualisation

One of the tricks I learned was to have every survey statement be answered with the same type of response. The likert-style scale is useful because it standardises the responses for rapid visualisation, and thus making meaning out of the data. It is

---

[2]

https://www.linkedin.com/pulse/getting-teams-evaluate-performance-greg-franklin/

typically a range of 5 replies, such as from "strongly disagree" to "strongly agree" or from "very dissatisfied" to "very satisfied". The responses I use in my survey are: Never, rarely, sometimes, often and always. Here is an example survey statement:

*Our pace of delivery is indefinitely sustainable; risk of burnout is low.*

## Visualise and communicate the results

The survey can be administered in a number of ways. I typically use Microsoft Forms or Google Forms. Once they've filled out the survey, you can use clever formulas to take all the responses and generate a visualisation by taking the number count of each response option for each survey question. The full survey can then be visualised as a heat map using colour coding for the responses.

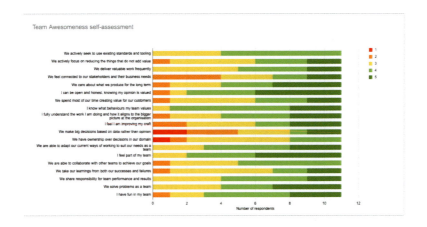

However, there is a crucial step that you mustn't leave out: review and discuss the results with the team!

You'd be amazed at how many team coaches leave this step out. I typically have a stand-alone session, which can be as short as 30 minutes. Once discussed and you understand which themes the team values, you can then align on what improvements to work on together.

## Let the team help decide what to take action on

During discussion of the results, I use facilitation techniques to find out which questions are important to the team, and which are less important. You can then find out whether a consensus can be reached on what area to work on. This is the moment where I typically am given permission to develop a short workshop to address the area of improvement.

Each item in the survey is associated with a theme. Themes can include psychological safety, company values, DevOps or Agile fundamentals. The example given above is related to the Agile Manifesto Principle number 8:

*Agile processes promote sustainable development. The sponsors, developers, and users should be able to maintain a constant pace indefinitely.*

## Keep the momentum by taking action

I typically like to develop, schedule and deliver a workshop to address the agreed-upon topic within a few weeks, so that we can form new habits as a team. This will give us some lead time to evolve before the next evaluation.

I typically run this kind of survey with a team every 3-6 months, depending on the desire for change. Running the survey again in the future is where things can get interesting. You can start to identify things that are trending up and trending down, and communicate them with the team.

*It is important to compare a team to their former selves, and not compare teams to each other.*

I don't recommend reporting a team's results to management. If multiple teams are involved, results can be rolled up and anonymised for purposes of departmental performance reporting, or to surface common themes.

**Try it yourself**

Anyone can design and run a team awesomeness survey by sticking to a few principles:

- Make it meaningful
- Design the survey in a practical way
- Visualise and communicate the results
- Let the team guide you on what is important
- Follow through and keep momentum

---

NB. The article has been republished with full permission from Greg.

# SPRINT 3

# SPRINT 3

Week 1

## Readiness

Check list
- Business alignment
- Value stream review
- Product Sync
- Team topology review

## Execution

Check list
- Scrum of Scrums / Coach sync
- 

## Reflection

Check list
- Team review(s)
- System demo
- Team Retro (s)
- Reporting

## Improvement

Check list
- Quarterly planning retro actions
- Team retro actions
-

Week 2

Readiness

Execution

Reflection

Improvement

# Business Alignment

In the book 'Drive', the author Dan Pink[1] states 3 factors involved in human motivation; Autonomy; Mastery; and Purpose. Specifically he defines purpose as:

> *"the yearning to do what we do in the service of something larger than ourselves."*

**In quarterly agile planning this is the shared vision and common goals everyone is working together to achieve.**

Without this you've just got a bunch of teams doing stuff, but you're probably not getting the best out of them or creating a motivating environment. To ensure this is not the case everyone needs clarity on how they contribute and what they are contributing to.

The business alignment session is there to review the high level strategy of the organisation, check if anything has changed and ensure that it's clear which part this group of interdependent teams are contributing to.

## The product or service being delivered should be directly aligned to at least one element of the strategy.

When the quarterly planning takes place there should be clear and evident articulation of this through both the backlog of work brought into the planning event, and from the objectives that emerge during it.

---

[1] https://www.danpink.com/books/drive/

# BUSINESS ALIGNMENT

## Useful questions
- Has anything changed with the strategy?
- Is it obvious what value we provide for the org?

## Logistics
- At least once per quarter
- Ensure everyone understands the strategic vision
- Ensure the programme backlog aligns with organisation direction / business goals

## Attendees
- Business Owner
- Product mgmt
- Tech leadership
- Exec Sponsor

## Inputs
- Strategic themes
- Business priorities

## Outcomes
- Alignment of your network of interdependent teams to company strategy

# VALUE STREAM MAPPING

## Useful questions
- Does this show every step of our process?
- Where are the hot spots?

## Outcomes
- An up-to-date value stream map
- Identified opportunities for reduction of waste

## Attendees
Representation from each group involved in the delivery of the product or service

## Logistics
- Once per quarter
- Facilitated by you!
- Ensure there is an end to end visual representation of your product or service

## Inputs
- Value stream maps
- Existing process flows

# 5 Reasons value stream mapping is a key tool

**The most common reason why quarterly agile planning fails to meet objectives? Misalignment of the interdependent teams, stakeholders, and the waste and inefficiency created.**

It's a common pitfall of trying to scale your business agility practices. I've seen this many times when teams are brought together to form a network of connected teams (an Agile Release Train in SAFe terms) when the reality is there's no real interdependencies, they're not working on a common product or service, and certainly not working from a shared backlog.

How to avoid it? Create and regularly review your value stream.

Value Stream Mapping (VSM) is a simple and super effective tool to help successfully create alignment. Put simply, it's the end-to-end visualisation of a product or service, and the bankable benefits are five-fold:

**1. Reduction of waste** (by identifying trouble spots in the process, or areas with significant wait times). By surfacing every step in a process, in the order they happen, the time they take, and the time between each step, you can interrogate the process and ask questions like:

- How long does each step take?
- Are there steps which can be removed?
- Are there steps which could happen in a different order?
- Are the right people responsible for the right things?
- Where is the highest wait time?

You quickly end up with a clear set of improvement opportunities to inform your backlog.

*"Value stream mapping helped our software development teams reduce lead time by 60%, reduce cycle time by 50%, and increase productivity by 20%."* Atlassian 2017

**2. Objective decision making on priorities.** Value stream mapping creates a clear visualisation to surface and understand the full system in play. Rather than considering aspects independently, you can take a holistic, systems view.

*"That's really an important aspect of value stream management, the idea that a business starts with an idea, but then it goes through a lot of different phases, a lot of different teams to actually deliver the value and realise the value. And the idea is to try to create that in a holistic view."* [Chris Condo, Forrester]

A holistic view is essential when you're trying to bring different teams together and understand their interdependence. There's something about the honesty and transparency of a visual map that removes emotion and subjective opinion. Instead providing a purely objective, dispassionate picture of what happens.

**3. Creates shared understanding.** Value stream mapping goes a long way to bringing teams together - it acts as referee mediating competing voices. Having everyone involved in doing the actual work directly contribute to the creation of the map generates a huge amount of energy and high levels of collaboration. It becomes a shared experience everyone will remember. Done well, it's true co-creation in action.

**4. Retention of knowledge** (getting stuff out of people's heads!) A huge factor undermining transformation - especially large multi-year endeavours - is staff attrition. When people move on, momentum and impetus wane, but also much of the knowledge and understanding gets lost too. This is why mapping is so critical. It gets information and knowledge out of people's brains and into a tangible artefact. It takes tacit knowledge and makes it explicit.

**5. It can support your strategic goals.** Value stream mapping has significant benefits when revisiting an existing product or service, as a tool for managing, measuring and keeping programs on track in the longer term. Identifying and mapping multiple value streams, identifying the common opportunities, the shared pain points and prioritising these according to your strategic objectives is where the magic really starts to happen.

This is one of the key tools to help clients focus on where they're trying to go - both at the beginning but more importantly into delivery, implementation and beyond. I've seen that it works and how it helps the adoption of a lean portfolio management approach.

# Quarterly planning is ongoing, with no final destination. Often what goes wrong is sustaining the energy beyond the initial excitement. Teams lose sight of where they're going.

Sure, value stream mapping[1] does a great job of bringing teams and silos together, getting them on the same page and helping share what they know and want. But it also does a fantastic job of pointing everyone towards the north star, and keeping them focussed on the opportunities for improvement.

So, urge your teams not to view it as a one-off exercise but as the creation of a living map, that's ever evolving as their landscape changes.

---

[1]

https://www.atlassian.com/continuous-delivery/principles/value-stream-mapping

# TEAM TOPOLOGY REVIEW

## Useful questions
- Have we defined the teams in the right way
- Where are most of our dependencies?
- Do we have a single backlog?
- Do we understand our interaction modes?

## Outcomes
- Agreement on optimal structure
- Agreed timeline for any changes

## Logistics
- Once per quarter
- Facilitated by you!
- Ensure the configuration and team design is optimised to support the value stream

## Attendees
- Scrum Masters
- Business Owner
- Tech leadership
- Product mgmt

## Inputs
- Existing teams
- Value stream map
- Knowledge of team topologies framework

# What is Team Topologies?

It's a book I strongly recommend because of its super helpful framework for designing and organising software development teams to optimise for fast delivery, high quality, and continuous improvement (that was quite a mouthful!).

It suggests four fundamental team types; Stream-aligned; Enabling; Complicated-subsystem; Platform and three team interaction modes; Collaboration; X-as-a-Service; Facilitating.

- **Stream-aligned** teams are responsible for delivering a specific product or service.
- **Enabling** teams provide specialised support like testing or security.
- **Complicated-subsystem** teams focus on a specific technical subsystem.
- **Platform** teams build and maintain a shared platform for other teams to use.

---

- **Collaboration interaction mode** emphasises close collaboration between teams.
- **X-as-a-Service interaction mode** focuses on providing a specific self-service capability to other teams.
- **Facilitating interaction mode** focuses on teams that support other teams through coaching, tooling, or other forms of facilitation.

The book also covers how to avoid common anti-patterns such as too many dependencies between teams or a lack of clear ownership for specific products or services.

**Once you have an up-to-date value stream map, the natural next step is to review your Team Topologies**[1].

---

[1] https://teamtopologies.com/

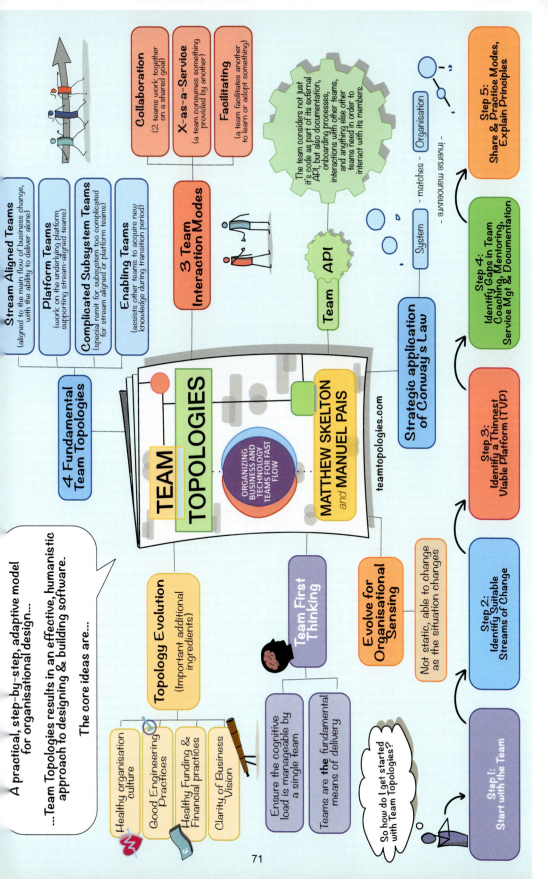

# SPRINT 4

# SPRINT 4           Week 1

## Readiness

Check list
- Funding allocation
- Training for new members / stakeholders

## Execution

Check list
- Scrum of Scrums / Coach sync
- Product Sync
- _____

## Reflection

Check list
- Team review(s)
- System demo
- Team Retro (s)
- Reporting

## Improvement

Check list
- Quarterly planning retro actions
- Team retro actions
- Communities of practice

# Week 2

Readiness

Execution

Reflection

Improvement

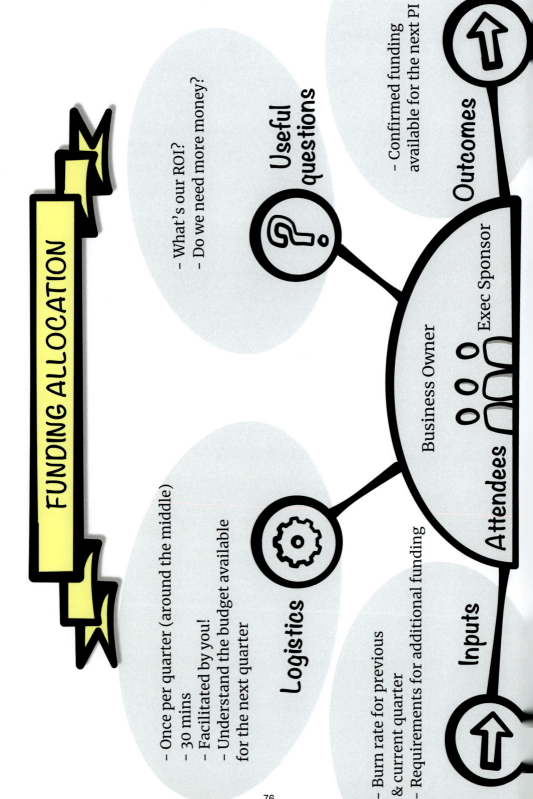

# Funding Allocation

**Even if you're not a budget holder yourself, this is still a conversation you need to ensure is happening on a regular basis.**

Regardless of whether the organisation has an annual funding cycle, you need visibility around how money is being spent, and to facilitate discussions with your stakeholders to determine what flexibility there is to manage how the budget is spent throughout the year.

This becomes particularly important when:

- You need to increase the number of people or teams required to deliver the product or service
- A decision is made to pivot which may require different individual skills or teams to be involved
- There are budget cuts being discussed
- New epics and features are being prioritised

Knowing the blended day rate for the different roles / team members within each interdependent team allows you to calculate the 'burn rate' i.e. how much is needed to pay for the people. You can then slice this per team, sprint and depending on the data available, even start to put a cost on feature delivery.

Gathering data and insights from the system demo (which should be happening each sprint by now) will help determine the return on investment (ROI).

The cost and the ROI should be the minimum criteria for any budget discussion.

## Bottom line - even if the total amount of money is set in stone, you should regularly review it with stakeholders and make adjustments on the allocation of the funding as necessary.

Don't make assumptions here or they may come back and bite you in the arse.

# SPRINT 5

# SPRINT 5

Week 1

## Readiness

**Check list**
- ○ Exec briefing prep
- ○ Product vision & feature backlog prep
- ○ Architecture vision prep
- ○ Event logistics check
- ○ Circulate agendas
- ○ Wrap up & reset prep

## Execution

**Check list**
- ○ Scrum of Scrums / Coach sync
- ○ ___

## Reflection

**Check list**
- ○ Team review(s)
- ○ System demo
- ○ Team Retro (s)
- ○ Reporting

## Improvement

**Check list**
- ○ Quarterly planning retro actions
- ○ Team retro actions
- ○ ___

# Week 2

Readiness

Execution

Reflection

Improvement

# WRAP UP & RESET

# WRAP UP & RESET   Week 1

## Readiness

**Check list**
- ⭘ Final quarterly planning prep
- ⭘ _____

## Execution

**Check list**
- ⭘ Innovation work
- ⭘ Hackathon
- ⭘ Quarterly planning

## Reflection

**Check list**
- ⭘ System demo
- ⭘ Quarterly business review
- ⭘ _____
- ⭘ _____

## Improvement

**Check list**
- ⭘ Quarterly planning retro
- ⭘ _____

Week 2

Readiness

Execution

Reflection

Improvement

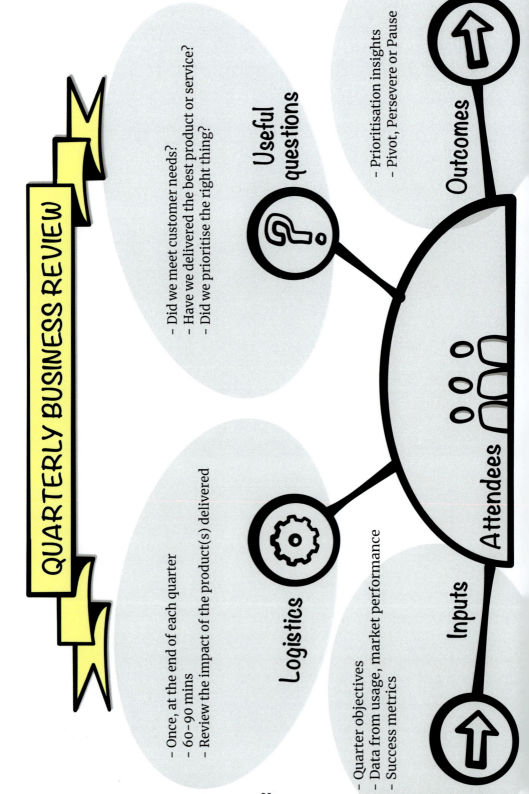

# Wrap up & Reset

At the end of each quarter your role is to help team members and stakeholders to press pause on the remote control.

Just like sprint reviews, retrospectives and planning at the team level, in order to understand what's happening; refine the process; get better; and ensure everyone is still aligned on the goal; there needs to be dedicated time for these discussions.

It reduces the risk of not focussing on objectives and work starting to expand and drift across multiple quarters. In the context of quarterly agile planning the concepts are identical, it's simply a case of scale.

## During the final two weeks there are 3 key things that need to happen before you start planning for the next quarter.

1. **Understand the output** of the quarter by showing working software or demonstrating a new / enhanced product. This is referred to in this journal as the **System Demo** (which should happen a few times during the quarter too - as suggested in the sprint's reflection checklists)

2. You then need to **map this to the objectives** and the intent articulated at the beginning of the quarter. You'll need to review the data and insights to tell the full story. How much

did we spend vs how much value did we get? Did we meet the goals? This is referred to in this journal as the **Quarterly Business Review**. It can take various forms and most often it's combined with the system demo.

My personal preference in a quarterly agile planning process is to make this a distinct event so there is absolute clarity on the purpose of each aspect. This way they get dedicated time and attention. It works well when there's an explicit start and end to the showing / discussing output and showing / discussing outcomes. But don't do one or the other. Do both in a way that works for you.

3. Then finally, step back from work and the value it's generated to **review the process**. The way the work gets done. The way communication happens. The people involved. This is referred to in this journal as the **Quarterly Retrospective**.

Now, it can be hard to facilitate a retrospective for up to 125 people. It's very different to a single team retro so you'll need to carefully consider the design and intent. Some ideas:

- **Use co facilitators** to spread the load and have smaller groups / breakouts working in parallel

- **Gather the data but sort out the actions later** - using a large wall or online whiteboard (Miro / Mural) spend the time together to extract information from the group around the themes you think are most appropriate

- **Pre-populate the data and just focus on actions**. Share the themes in advance and provide a space for people to add their ideas before the retrospective. Then use the time together to decide what improvement actions to prioritise and find owners

- **Use the team's sprint retrospective actions** as the agenda. Spend the time to collate the themes that emerged from all of the teams during the quarter, then during the retrospective ask the teams to pick a theme that was raised by another team and come up with a way to improve or avoid it

- **Hypothesis / Experiment design** - in small groups you can encourage this problem solving approach by having them use an experiment canvas (see next page)

*"Teams that make experimentation a core part of their culture create a competitive advantage, because they're able to make better decisions and innovations faster than those that don't."*
Stefan Thomke's HBR article "The Discipline of Business Experimentation"[1]

---

[1] https://hbr.org/2014/12/the-discipline-of-business-experimentation

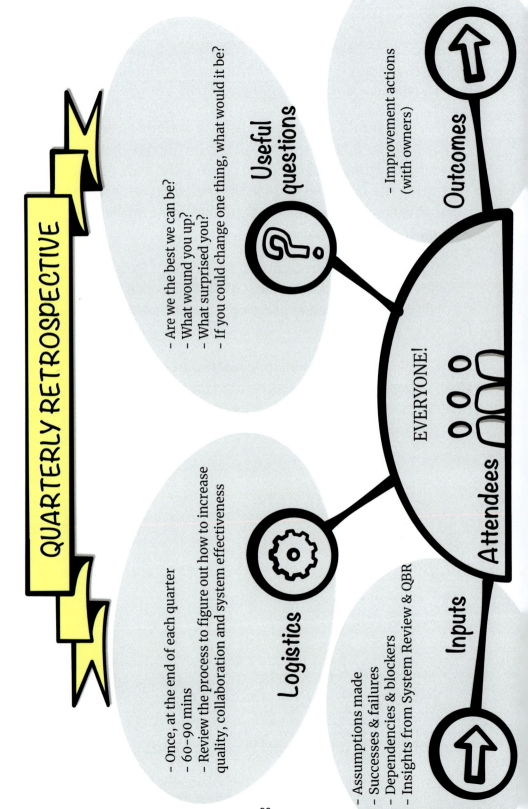

# EXPERIMENT CANVAS

| Title: | Leader(s): | Start: | End: |

## CONTEXT
The problem, challenge or opportunity is...

## HYPOTHESIS
Construct your hypothesis

We believe <this idea>

Will result in <this outcome>

We'll have confidence to proceed when <we see this measurable signal>

## EXPERIMENT SETUP
What will you actually do?
Who do you need to run the experiment?
How many times will you run it?

## CONSTRAINTS
Our constraints to run the experiment are...

## HIGHER INTENT
This helps the business to...

## RESULTS
The qualitative or quantitative results are...

## CONCLUSION
Did your results match your hypothesis?
What does this mean?

☐ VALIDATED
☐ INVALIDATED
☐ INCONCLUSIVE

## NEXT STEPS
Our next move is...
The decisions or actions we can now make are...

# The Main Event

This is it. The big one.

Despite so many different events throughout each quarter, the planning event is the nucleus. This is where you set the teams up for success over the next 3 months through a shared planning process, aligned around common goals.

My main advice? **Ask for help.**

Whether it's from agile coaches, Scrum Masters, Release Train Engineers or external consultants, it's almost impossible to design and run this event if you're flying solo. There's absolutely no shame in requesting some support. In fact it actually models the right level of vulnerability and behaviour.

Be aware that some people may be resistant at first. On face value a multi-day planning event for 50 - 125 people sounds flipping expensive and a potential waste of precious development time. But it creates something intangible. An energy and intrinsic value that is difficult to measure. It provides a space to create:

- **A sense of cohesion** – when asking the question "What's the biggest benefit of the quarterly planning event you experienced" the most common answer I've received is "Feeling part of something bigger"

- **A common purpose** – a key human motivator is purpose so whether or not every team is working from a single backlog, they should all be working for the same cause. There's no better time to align people than when they're in front of you

- **An initial connection** – to put faces to names and voices, to observe the different size and make up of each team

- **A deeper connection** – being able to look someone in the eye, read their body language, see how their breathing changes in certain circumstances, to taste the same food, to experience the same weather, builds a stronger relationship in 2 days than you can ever get in weeks or even months of talking to someone on the phone

- **Tribes beyond your immediate team** – with large group facilitation techniques, individuals can quickly find common ground with others they may never have spoken to before

- **Reinforce / Build culture** – lots of discreet things can contribute to the culture of the event but also the longer term vibe of how you work and interact (agenda / timings / common language / consistent messaging)

- **Psychological safety** – forming an alliance for the event, openly encouraging and recognising leadership, presence, honesty and vulnerability allows for acknowledgement of good behaviours, and open conversations about what can be improved. This is hugely powerful when not done behind the scenes, and helps everyone understand the boundaries within which they're working.

The event provides the opportunity, but the list above doesn't happen by magic. Whomever is organising and running the event (yeah, that's you!) has to make a deliberate effort to foster these points. To step back from following a process and focus on the individuals. To create activities, facilitate events and arrange the space to encourage and support them.

The amount of time needed for the event depends on how many people are involved, and the maturity i.e. how many times they've done this before. If you're all in person then 2 days should be ample time, if it's remote across multi-time zones then you will probably need to split this across 3 days.

# It sounds romantic I know, but with the right intention and execution your quarterly agile planning events can actually become quite special, maybe even something your colleagues look forward to and enjoy...

Setting the agenda[1] is up to you, but typically includes this kind of stuff happens on the first day:

- Exec sponsor and/or senior stakeholder share high level strategic goals for next 12-18 months
- Product management share the product or service vision for the next 12-18 months
- Product owners share the prioritised product outcomes for the next 3-6 months
- Quarterly agile planner / RTE / Agile coach shares any constraints / considerations teams need to be aware of
- Teams then breakout and plan out the features and stories that support the delivery of value

Typically this stuff happens at the end:

- Teams present back objectives and high level plans
- Sponsors and stakeholders confirm the value
- Quarterly agile planner / RTE / Agile coach shares the dependencies and risks surfaced during the planning

---

[1] https://www.sessionlab.com/blog/quarterly-planning-workshop/
https://www.dockethq.com/resources/quarterly-planning-meeting/
https://scaledagileframework.com/pi-planning/

**Some bonus facilitation ideas for the quarterly planning event:**

- **Bingo** - to help the group stay attentive during the day 1 Business context and product vision sections (let's face it not everyone is engaging public speakers), create and distribute bingo cards with related content e.g. jargon, Agile BS[2], or key words you know will come up in the presentations. Have small prizes for who completes the first line and the full card.

- **Constellations** - If you're in the same physical space it's simply too good an opportunity to miss.[3]

- **Different voices** - Encourage different people to contribute rather than hearing the same people all the time

- **Social event** - having some kind of social event in the evening between day 1 and 2 is a great way to deepen connection outside of the 'formal' setting

- **10% Oxygen boost** - I love this one. Every 20 minutes during the business context and product vision, simply ask everyone to stand up for 10 seconds. Explain that we can typically concentrate for around 20 mins, and that simply by standing up you give the brain a 10% oxygen boost.

- **Pecha Kucha** - introduce a novel presentation format to keep things fresh. Poster on next page

- **Don't start from scratch** - check out the Quarterly business review template in Miro[4], the PI Planning event guidance[5] on the SAFe website and ask your peers for advice and guidance on what works (and what doesn't!)

---

[2] https://www.noelwarnell.uk/post/agile-bullshit
[3] https://www.sessionlab.com/methods/constellations
[4] https://miro.com/templates/qbr-presentation/
[5] https://scaledagileframework.com/pi-planning/

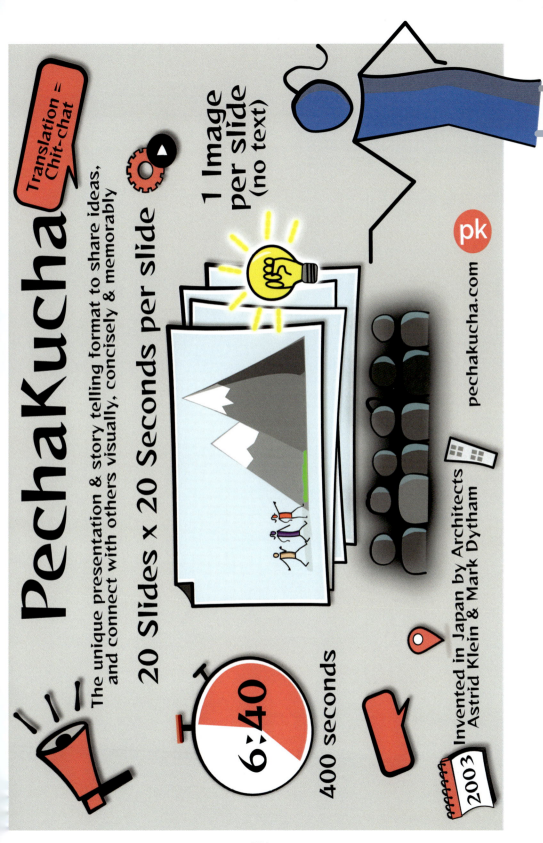

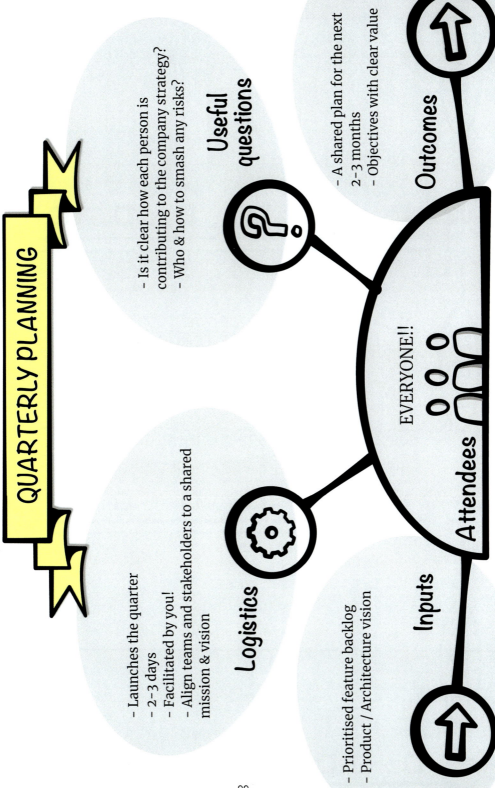

Quarterly planning checklist for: _____

# You! The Quarterly Agile Planner

## BEFORE

- ☐ **Confirm cadence** – Provide the schedule for the upcoming quarter and sprint dates
- ☐ **Coach** – Ensure scrum masters are ready, leaders know the purpose / outcome, team members understand the planning process
- ☐ **Schedule events** – ensure the right calendar invites have gone to the right people
- ☐ **Agree measures** – work with Product manager, Tech Lead, stakeholders and Scrum Masters to agree how to measure success
- ☐ **Manage expectations** – Ensure everyone understands the outcome is an intention rather than a promise, and that predictability is variable, (don't load up all sprints!).
- ☐ **Seek support** – from an agile coach or a co-facilitator to help organise & run the event
- ☐ **Cater for people** (not just process) – ensure regular breaks & time zones are considered. Are there activities to connect people on a human level & to have fun during the event?
- ☐ **Rehearse** – organise a presentations dry run prior. Do this collectively to ensure consistent messaging and avoid surprises.
- ☐ **Seek a balance** – planning should not only consider business demand, but any technical demand, release activities, product support that will absorb capacity during the PI

## DURING

- ☐ **Open the event** – As the central organiser for the planning event everyone is looking to you to guide the event and provide clear guidance on what needs to happen, and when. Starting with the opening on day 1.
- ☐ **Facilitate Scrum of Scrums** – Bring the Scrum Master's together at regular intervals to coach the planning process and encourage visibility of progress, blockers, risks and dependencies.
- ☐ **Unblock** – As you become aware of any challenges emerging for the teams help to resolve these as quickly as possible during the event by co-coordinating discussions or bringing it the right people to the right conversation
- ☐ **Float** – ensure everyone knows how to contact you at any point during the event. Pop into the team discussions and check in with stakeholders regularly.
- ☐ **Protect the teams** – ensure they are not being asked to over commit (or doing that to themselves) or plan unrefined work that isn't 'Ready'
- ☐ **Close the event** – facilitate the plan reviews, and encourage discussion and feedback from stakeholders

## AFTER

- ☐ **Consult** – ensure regular communication is happening, and that you're aligned on current and future aspirations
- ☐ **Facilitate Scrum of Scrums** – Bring the Scrum Master's together at regular intervals to coach the quarterly agile planning process and encourage visibility of progress, blockers, risks and dependencies.
- ☐ **Attend sprint reviews** – to understand progress, encourage interaction with stakeholders and understand what may need to be included in the end of quarter system review
- ☐ **Focus on continuous improvement** – identify trends, gather empirical data and work with the train towards improving predictability, quality and enjoyment
- ☐ **Measure progress** – at any point during the qtr you should be able to provide information based on the objectives and associated business value achieved to date

# Quarterly planning checklist for: Scrum Master / Team Coach

## BEFORE

- **Capacity** – Know team members availability for each sprint considering national holidays, scheduled vacations, planned leavers / joiners
- **Velocity** – Know the average amount of work that the team completes each sprint
- **Events** – checked for any release dates, maintenance work, marketing activity happening within the PI
- **Collaboration** – work with PO to understand the business priorities for the qtr. Help the PO understand any technical enabler work required within the qtr
- **DoR / DoD** – Document and ensure everyone has visibility of your definition of ready (work is at a suitable level of granularity to plan into a sprint), and definition of done (what triggers work to be classified as completed)

Download at noelwarnell.uk/QAP

## DURING

- **Guide the team re appropriate level of detail** – first 2 sprints should be planned with stories up to 80% of available capacity. Sprint 3–5 with features you intend to start.
- **Identify dependencies** – record anything you need from anyone external to the team to complete work during the qtr. Raise these during Scrum of Scrums meetings and try to agree them during the planning event
- **Identify Risks** – record anything that could negatively impact the teams ability to complete the objectives. ROAM format.
- **Collaboration** – work with the PO to articulate the objectives for the team, for the qtr.
- **Visibility** – Ensure the teams plan, dependencies and risk are available to everybody throughout the planning process
- **Attend Scrum of Scrums** – Represent the team in regular meetings with other Scrum masters. Escalate blockers, seek advice and help needed
- **Facilitate confidence vote** – at regular intervals ask the team - "Are we confident with this plan?". Towards the end of the planning take a score from each team member from 1 (lowest) to 5 (highest confidence)
- **Present** – back the high level plan at the end of the planning event (with PO and Team)

## AFTER

- **Protect the team** – by providing ongoing transparency of progress, blockers, dependencies to stakeholders and honouring the DoR / DoD
- **Attend Scrum of Scrums** – Represent the team in regular meetings with other Scrum masters for the train. Escalating blockers and seeking advice and help as appropriate.
- **Maintain the sprint cadence** – schedule the sprint events (Planning / Daily Scrum / Review / Retrospective) and ensure invites are available to relevant participants. These events are not optional.
- **Focus on continuous improvement** – identify trends, gather empirical data and work with the team towards improving predictability, quality and enjoyment
- **Measure progress** – at any point during the quarter you should be able to provide information based on the objectives and associated business value achieved to date for the team

# Quarterly planning checklist for: Product Owner

## BEFORE

- [ ] **Share product vision** – ensure you are able to articulate the product vision (of the product manager) to the team
- [ ] **Feature refinement** – Ensure there is a backlog of features that align with the priorities of the Product vision (provided by the product manager)
- [ ] **Story refinement** – Ensure there is a backlog of stories that meet the DoR criteria for at least 2 sprints
- [ ] **Maintain the backlog** – through the above refinement and also constant collaboration with product managers around priorities
- [ ]

## DURING

- [ ] **Plan** – Work with the team to create sprint goals, high level sprint plans and clarify backlog items
- [ ] **Collaborate** – with the team to form PI objectives and ensure the planning compliments these. With other product owners to co-ordinate dependencies through backlog ordering
- [ ] **Present** – back the high level plan at the end of the PI planning event (along with the SM and the Team)
- [ ]
- [ ]

## AFTER

- [ ] **Facilitate sprint reviews** – At the end of each sprint the PO should be articulating to stakeholders the intention of the sprint, what progress was made toward PI objectives, provide transparency of any blockers and seek feedback
- [ ] **Maintain the backlog** – through refinement and constant collaboration with product managers around priorities
- [ ] **Provide sign-off** – Continuously accept / reject completed stories
- [ ] **Be available** – Is available to the team every day to answer questions and clarify stories
- [ ] **Measure value** – Meet regularly with the product manager to keep them informed of how much value is being generated, and prioritise future work.
- [ ]

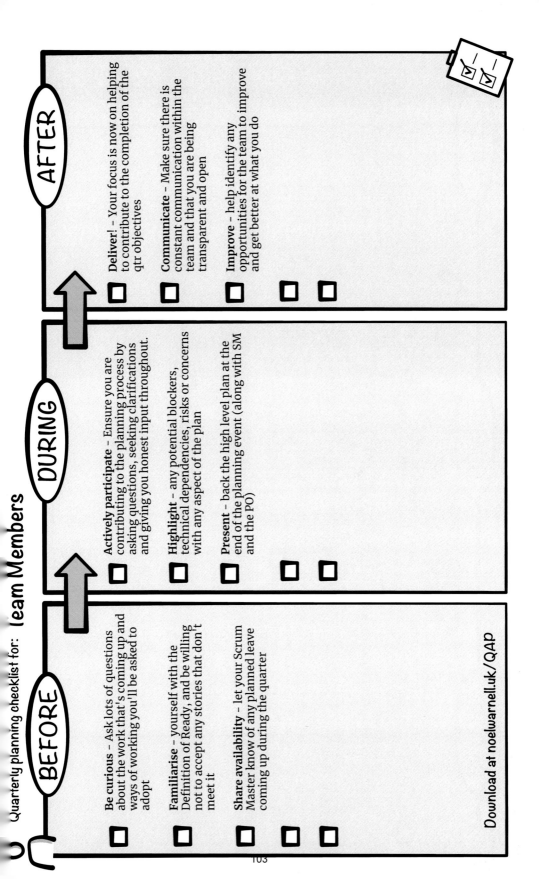

# Quarterly planning checklist for: Tech Leadership / System Architect

## BEFORE

- ☐ **Collaborate** – Work with the Product Manager to ensure technical enablers are properly prioritised so as not to introduce debt into the system. Also working with developers in the teams to ensure no surprises.

- ☐ **Create Technical vision and roadmap** – needs to be created and maintained, whilst aligning to any strategic direction or goals. You should be able to articulate this in both short term (current qtr) and medium term (Next 2–3 qtr) perspectives.

- ☐ **Maintain the funnel** – ensuring there is a prioritised and refined backlog of technical requirements

- ☐ **Rehearse** – participate in a dry run of any presentations prior to the planning event. Ideally this is done collectively to ensure consistent messaging and avoid surprises.

- ☐

## DURING

- ☐ **Present** – the technical vision, road map and priority backlog items
- ☐ **Be available** – to the teams to answer questions
- ☐
- ☐
- ☐

## AFTER

- ☐ **Consult** – ensure regular communication is happening, and that you're aligned on, and aligning others on current and future aspirations
- ☐
- ☐

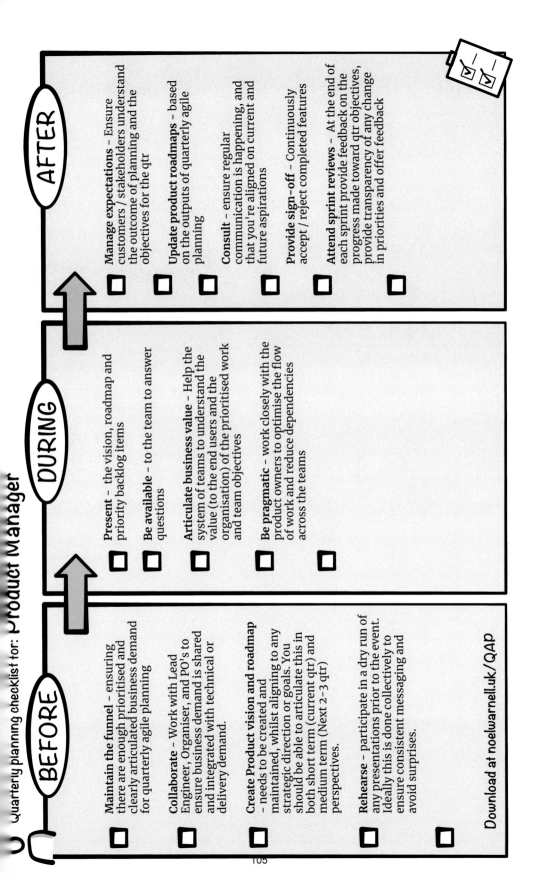

# Q2

*"Companies with quarterly planning cycles had a 20% higher annual growth rate than those with longer planning cycles. In addition, these companies had a 14% higher profitability and a 14% higher customer retention rate."*

Aberdeen Group: November 2015

# SPRINT 1

# SPRINT 1

Week 1

## Readiness

**Check list**
- ☐ Send placeholder invites for next quarterly planning event
- ☐ Send invites for System events for this quarter

## Execution

**Check list**
- ☐ Scrum of Scrums / Coach sync
- ☐ Product Sync
- ☐ _____

## Reflection

**Check list**
- ☐ Team review(s)
- ☐ System demo
- ☐ Team Retro (s)
- ☐ _____

## Improvement

**Check list**
- ☐ Quarterly planning retro actions
- ☐ _____

Week 2

Readiness

Execution

Reflection

Improvement

# SPRINT 2

# SPRINT 2

Week 1

## Readiness

**Check list**
- ☐ Next quarterly planning event venue / meeting room booking
- ☐ _____

## Execution

**Check list**
- ☐ Scrum of Scrums / Coach sync
- ☐ Product Sync
- ☐ _____

## Reflection

**Check list**
- ☐ Team review(s)
- ☐ System demo
- ☐ Team Retro (s)
- ☐ Reporting

## Improvement

**Check list**
- ☐ Quarterly planning retro actions
- ☐ Team retro actions
- ☐ Communities of practice

# Week 2

**Readiness**

---

**Execution**

---

**Reflection**

---

**Improvement**

# SPRINT 3

# SPRINT 3    Week 1

## Readiness

**Check list**
- ○ Business alignment
- ○ Value stream review
- ○ Product Sync
- ○ Team topology review

## Execution

**Check list**
- ○ Scrum of Scrums / Coach sync
- ○ ___

## Reflection

**Check list**
- ○ Team review(s)
- ○ System demo
- ○ Team Retro (s)
- ○ Reporting

## Improvement

**Check list**
- ○ Quarterly planning retro actions
- ○ Team retro actions
- ○ ___

# Week 2

Readiness

Execution

Reflection

Improvement

# SPRINT 4

# SPRINT 4    Week 1

## Readiness

Check list
- Funding allocation
- Training for new members / stakeholders

## Execution

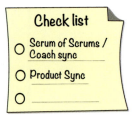

Check list
- Scrum of Scrums / Coach sync
- Product Sync
- _____

## Reflection

Check list
- Team review(s)
- System demo
- Team Retro (s)
- Reporting

## Improvement

Check list
- Quarterly planning retro actions
- Team retro actions
- Communities of practice

Week 2

Readiness

Execution

Reflection

Improvement

# SPRINT 5

# SPRINT 5  Week 1

## Readiness

**Check list**
- ☐ Exec briefing prep
- ☐ Product vision & feature backlog prep
- ☐ Architecture vision prep
- ☐ Event logistics check
- ☐ Circulate agendas
- ☐ Wrap up & reset prep

## Execution

**Check list**
- ☐ Scrum of Scrums / Coach sync
- ☐ _____

## Reflection

**Check list**
- ☐ Team review(s)
- ☐ System demo
- ☐ Team Retro (s)
- ☐ Reporting

## Improvement

**Check list**
- ☐ Quarterly planning retro actions
- ☐ Team retro actions
- ☐ _____

Week 2

Readiness

Execution

Reflection

Improvement

# WRAP UP & RESET

# WRAP UP & RESET

Week 1

## Readiness

**Check list**
- ○ Final quarterly planning prep
- ○ _____

## Execution

**Check list**
- ○ Innovation work
- ○ Hackathon
- ○ Quarterly planning

## Reflection

**Check list**
- ○ System demo
- ○ Quarterly business review
- ○ _____
- ○ _____

## Improvement

**Check list**
- ○ Quarterly planning retro
- ○ _____

# Week 2

Readiness

Execution

Reflection

Improvement

# Q3

*"companies using quarterly planning had a 70% higher likelihood of achieving their financial targets than those that didn't."*

Boston Consulting Group: 2018

# SPRINT 1

# SPRINT 1

Week 1

## Readiness

- Send placeholder invites for next quarterly planning event
- Send invites for System events for this quarter

## Execution

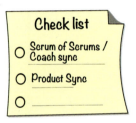

- Scrum of Scrums / Coach sync
- Product Sync
- _____

## Reflection

- Team review(s)
- System demo
- Team Retro (s)
- _____

## Improvement

- Quarterly planning retro actions
- _____

Week 2

Readiness

Execution

Reflection

Improvement

# SPRINT 2

# SPRINT 2

Week 1

## Readiness

**Check list**
- ☐ Next quarterly planning event venue / meeting room booking
- ☐ _____

## Execution

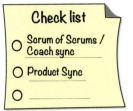

**Check list**
- ☐ Scrum of Scrums / Coach sync
- ☐ Product Sync
- ☐ _____

## Reflection

**Check list**
- ☐ Team review(s)
- ☐ System demo
- ☐ Team Retro (s)
- ☐ Reporting

## Improvement

**Check list**
- ☐ Quarterly planning retro actions
- ☐ Team retro actions
- ☐ Communities of practice

Week 2

Readiness

Execution

Reflection

Improvement

# SPRINT 3

# SPRINT 3           Week 1

## Readiness

**Check list**
- ○ Business alignment
- ○ Value stream review
- ○ Product Sync
- ○ Team topology review

## Execution

**Check list**
- ○ Scrum of Scrums / Coach sync
- ○ _____

## Reflection

**Check list**
- ○ Team review(s)
- ○ System demo
- ○ Team Retro (s)
- ○ Reporting

## Improvement

**Check list**
- ○ Quarterly planning retro actions
- ○ Team retro actions
- ○ _____

Week 2

Readiness

Execution

Reflection

Improvement

# SPRINT 4

# SPRINT 4

Week 1

## Readiness

Check list
- Funding allocation
- Training for new members / stakeholders

## Execution

Check list
- Scrum of Scrums / Coach sync
- Product Sync
- 

## Reflection

Check list
- Team review(s)
- System demo
- Team Retro (s)
- Reporting

## Improvement

Check list
- Quarterly planning retro actions
- Team retro actions
- Communities of practice

# Week 2

**Readiness**

**Execution**

**Reflection**

**Improvement**

# SPRINT 5

# SPRINT 5

Week 1

## Readiness

**Check list**
- ☐ Exec briefing prep
- ☐ Product vision & feature backlog prep
- ☐ Architecture vision prep
- ☐ Event logistics check
- ☐ Circulate agendas
- ☐ Wrap up & reset prep

## Execution

**Check list**
- ☐ Scrum of Scrums / Coach sync
- ☐ _____

## Reflection

**Check list**
- ☐ Team review(s)
- ☐ System demo
- ☐ Team Retro (s)
- ☐ Reporting

## Improvement

**Check list**
- ☐ Quarterly planning retro actions
- ☐ Team retro actions
- ☐ _____

Week 2

Readiness

Execution

Reflection

Improvement

# WRAP UP & RESET

# WRAP UP & RESET   Week 1

## Readiness

**Check list**
- ☐ Final quarterly planning prep
- ☐ _____

## Execution

**Check list**
- ☐ Innovation work
- ☐ Hackathon
- ☐ Quarterly planning

## Reflection

**Check list**
- ☐ System demo
- ☐ Quarterly business review
- ☐ _____
- ☐ _____

## Improvement

**Check list**
- ☐ Quarterly planning retro
- ☐ _____

Week 2

Readiness

Execution

Reflection

Improvement

# Q4

*"88% of companies reported that they were better able to adapt to change with quarterly planning. 78% of companies reported that quarterly planning improved collaboration between departments."*

Adaptive Insights CFO Indicator Q2 report 2018

# SPRINT 1

# SPRINT 1    Week 1

## Readiness

**Check list**
- Send placeholder invites for next quarterly planning event
- Send invites for System events for this quarter

## Execution

**Check list**
- Scrum of Scrums / Coach sync
- Product Sync
- _____

## Reflection

**Check list**
- Team review(s)
- System demo
- Team Retro (s)
- _____

## Improvement

**Check list**
- Quarterly planning retro actions
- _____

Week 2

Readiness

Execution

Reflection

Improvement

# SPRINT 2

# SPRINT 2

Week 1

## Readiness

**Check list**
- Next quarterly planning event venue / meeting room booking
- _____

## Execution

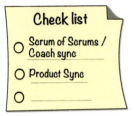
**Check list**
- Scrum of Scrums / Coach sync
- Product Sync
- _____

## Reflection

**Check list**
- Team review(s)
- System demo
- Team Retro (s)
- Reporting

## Improvement

**Check list**
- Quarterly planning retro actions
- Team retro actions
- Communities of practice

# Week 2

Readiness

Execution

Reflection

Improvement

# SPRINT 3

# SPRINT 3          Week 1

## Readiness

**Check list**
- ○ Business alignment
- ○ Value stream review
- ○ Product Sync
- ○ Team topology review

## Execution

**Check list**
- ○ Scrum of Scrums / Coach sync
- ○ 

## Reflection

**Check list**
- ○ Team review(s)
- ○ System demo
- ○ Team Retro (s)
- ○ Reporting

## Improvement

**Check list**
- ○ Quarterly planning retro actions
- ○ Team retro actions
- ○

# Week 2

Readiness

Execution

Reflection

Improvement

# SPRINT 4

# SPRINT 4

Week 1

## Readiness

Check list
- Funding allocation
- Training for new members / stakeholders

## Execution

Check list
- Scrum of Scrums / Coach sync
- Product Sync
- _____

## Reflection

Check list
- Team review(s)
- System demo
- Team Retro (s)
- Reporting

## Improvement

Check list
- Quarterly planning retro actions
- Team retro actions
- Communities of practice

# Week 2

Readiness

Execution

Reflection

Improvement

# SPRINT 5

# SPRINT 5

Week 1

## Readiness

**Check list**
- Exec briefing prep
- Product vision & feature backlog prep
- Architecture vision prep
- Event logistics check
- Circulate agendas
- Wrap up & reset prep

## Execution

**Check list**
- Scrum of Scrums / Coach sync
- 

## Reflection

**Check list**
- Team review(s)
- System demo
- Team Retro (s)
- Reporting

## Improvement

**Check list**
- Quarterly planning retro actions
- Team retro actions
-

# Week 2

Readiness

Execution

Reflection

Improvement

# WRAP UP & RESET

# WRAP UP & RESET     Week 1

## Readiness

Check list
- Final quarterly planning prep
- ___

## Execution

Check list
- Innovation work
- Hackathon
- Quarterly planning

## Reflection

Check list
- System demo
- Quarterly business review
- ___
- ___

## Improvement

Check list
- Quarterly planning retro
- ___

# Week 2

## Readiness

## Execution

## Reflection

## Improvement

# What's next?

Well, that's really up to you. But remember:

*Scaling is not the goal.*

Nor is doing LeSS, being SAFe or a good DAD[1]. If you've got no idea what I'm on about, these are ~~cash cows~~ frameworks for scaling agile.

They're designed with good intentions to help provide structure and guidance on how to do stuff (typically software delivery) across multiple teams and departments quickly and logically in order to deliver value to customers.

Now the problem is this – because of the highly prescriptive nature of each framework it's easy to become engrossed and maybe even a little obsessed with doing it. On being able to demonstrate that it's being followed 'correctly'. On taking the suggestions literally and trying to apply all of them to the letter (and lambasting anyone that dares to step outside of the guidelines).
However, this means that we lose sight of what is actually important.

## These frameworks in themselves are not the goal.

As long as we remember to see them for what they are – tools that *may* be able to help us realise our business goals (depending on your specific context), we are going to be OK. But lose sight of the real goal of delivering value to customers and/or internal stakeholders and we're in trouble. Yet all too often we fall into this trap.

---

[1] https://less.works/
https://scaledagileframework.com/
https://www.pmi.org/disciplined-agile/process/introduction-to-dad

We (and the organisations we work with) start to focus on the rules of the game. We start to see following the framework as success. We think we're winning because on paper we tick the boxes of doing the meetings, having the right buzzwords and changing the names of people's roles. What a shame. We couldn't be farther from the truth.

Successful agile transformations happen REGARDLESS of the framework used. And so does successful delivery of value to customers. They happen by:

- Having leaders who can align people to a shared goal
- Having a group of people willing to experiment with new ideas
- Not having a fear of failure
- A commitment to constant improvement
- Creating an environment of trust and psychological safety
- Allowing people the space to focus, have autonomy and achieve mastery (if they so desire)
- Putting the right people in the right roles

**Ultimately it comes down to the simple question – what's the point? Why is it that your organisation desires becoming more agile? What's the problem that you are trying to solve? Who for?** *That's* **your goal. Make sure everyone understands it. But does it matter how you get there? It might, but how you choose to get there needs to be right for your context.**

Whoop whoop, you made it to the end! Nice one.

I welcome any feedback to improve The Quarterly Agile Planning Journal.

If you found it useful it would make my day if you could share a photo of you and the book on LinkedIn, and tag me in.

Also, did you know that a fairy dies every time you read a book but don't leave a review on Amazon? Crazy...

Anyway, thank you for choosing this book, I appreciate you. Noel.

## Author Bio

Noel Warnell is an experienced Agile practitioner with a potent creative streak. With over 200 written articles, over 50 visual book summaries, this is his second self-publication.

He is currently the Director of Agile Delivery at Reason, helping businesses to make things better.

His work is centred around helping teams, executives and organisations to design, implement and evolve their agile strategy. Recent clients include Deutsche Bank, Levis, Wall Street English, Diageo and DK Publishing.

Noel is also a professional 1-1 coach (ICF PCC), a BIMA mentor and has been running the monthly 'Facilitation Lab' event with Tobias Mayer since 2018.

Outside of work he's a married father of 3 teenagers, with 2 dogs, living in London, and you can easily get him excited by talking about books.

Find out more https://www.noelwarnell.uk/
Connect via www.linkedin.com/in/noelwarnell/
Send an email to work@noelwarnell.uk